The Soccer Math Book

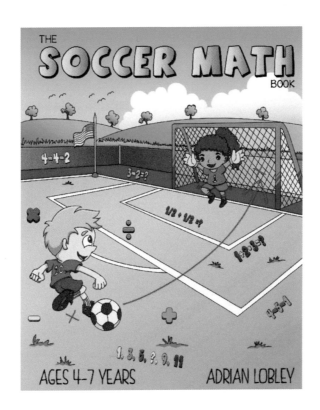

Adrian Lobley

To Sebastian

With thanks to:
Sebastian Wraith-Lobley
Sarah Wraith
Ian Core
Steve Wright
Simon Brooksbank
Joshua Clements
Christopher Chamberlain
Hayden Cowan
Finlay Cronshaw
and
Miss Pugh

Front/back cover illustrations by:
Alyssa Josue

Fill in the missing numbers on the shirts.

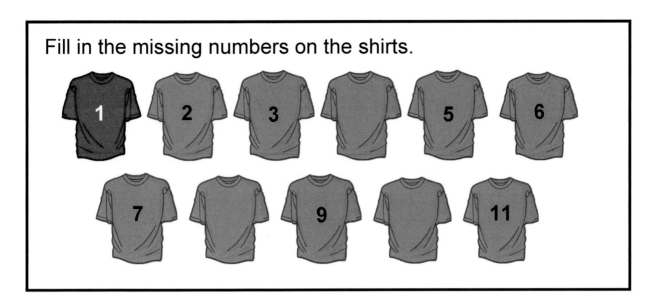

 The goalkeeper always wears a different colored shirt

Well done! Let's try this exercise one more time...

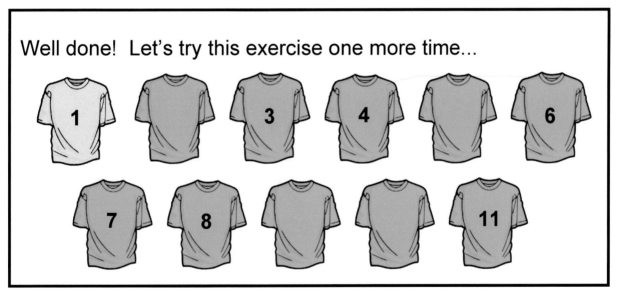

Write your match score for this page by entering the number of shirts you got right and wrong here: ☐ — ☐

Below is an 11-a-side team. The players who wear these shirts tend to stay in that position on the soccer field. Draw a line from the highest number, 11 to 10, then link 10 to 9 and continue down to 1.

Attackers

10   9

Midfielders

11   4   8   7

Defenders

3   5   6   2

Goalkeeper

1

Write your match score for this page by entering the number of links you got right and wrong here: ☐ — ☐

If a player scores 3 goals in a match, this is called a **hat-trick**

If a player scores a **hat-trick** in his first match and then 2 goals in his next match, how many goals has the player scored in total?

   +

3 + 2 = ☐

If a player scores 1 goal in his first match and then a **hat-trick** in his second match, how many goals has he scored?

 +

1 + 3 = ☐

Write your match score for this page by entering the number of questions you got right and wrong here: ☐ — ☐

3

In a 4-a-side match, there are 2 teams with 4 players in each team. How many players are there in total?

4 + 4 = ☐

In a 7-a-side match, how many players are there in total?

7 + 7 = ☐

Enter your match score for this page: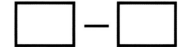

Use the number line below to help you with this question

If a team wins 4-1 then they have won by 3 goals because 4 - 1 = 3

How many goals did the following teams win by?

Dallas   won   3 – 1   ☐

Chicago   won   4 – 3   ☐

Houston   won   3 – 2   ☐

```
0   1   2   3   4   5   6
|   |   |   |   |   |   |
```

How many goals did the following teams win by?

Orlando   won   2 – 0   ☐

Seattle   won   6 – 3   ☐

New York   won   5 – 2   ☐

Enter your score for the 6 questions above: ☐ — ☐

If a cup match finishes as a draw then the 2 teams often contest a penalty shoot-out, to find out who the winner will be.

A cup match is a one-off match between 2 teams

A green circle = penalty scored.

A red circle = penalty missed.

Below Chicago have 2 green circles and 3 red circles so they scored 2 penalties. Enter in the box the number of penalties Seattle scored.

Chicago ⚫ ⚪ ⚫ ⚪ ⚫ = 2

Seattle ⚪ ⚫ ⚪ ⚫ ⚪ =

Which team won?

Both boxes correct? Enter your score: ☐ — ☐

What is the penalty shoot-out score here?

New York ⚫ ⚪ ⚫ ⚪ ⚪ = ☐

Portland ⚪ ⚪ ⚫ ⚪ ⚪ = ☐

Which team won? ☐

What is the penalty shoot-out score here?

Houston ⚫ ⚫ ⚪ ⚪ ⚫ = ☐

Dallas ⚪ ⚫ ⚪ ⚫ ⚪ = ☐

Which team won? ☐

All 6 boxes correct? Enter your score: ☐ — ☐

One Dallas player scored a hat-trick (i.e. 3 goals) in one of these 3 matches. Which match did he score the hat-trick in? Tick the only box it can be.

Dallas 1 – 2 New York ☐
Dallas 3 – 1 Portland ☐
Dallas 0 – 1 Orlando ☐

One Orlando player scored a hat-trick in one of these matches. Which match did he score the hat-trick in?

Orlando 1 – 1 Houston ☐
Orlando 0 – 2 Columbus ☐
Orlando 4 – 2 Seattle ☐

Enter your score for this page: ☐ – ☐

Cross out half (½) of the soccer balls in each set below. Enter the number remaining.

⚽ ⚽ ⚽   ⚽ ⚽ ⚽ ⚽

⚽ ⚽ ⚽ ☐   ⚽⚽ ⚽ ⚽ ☐

How many players are there in the picture below? ☐

Cross out half (½) of the players.

How many players remain? ☐

Enter your score for this page: ☐ — ☐

Keep doubling the score below.

↓ | 2 | – | 1 | ↓

| | – | |

| | – | |

Double the scores below, in the boxes opposite.

| 4 | – | 0 | ⟹ | | – | |

| 0 | – | 0 | ⟹ | | – | |

| 1 | – | 1 | ⟹ | | – | |

| 2 | – | 2 | ⟹ | | – | |

| 1 | – | 3 | ⟹ | | – | |

Enter your score for this page: | | — | |

10

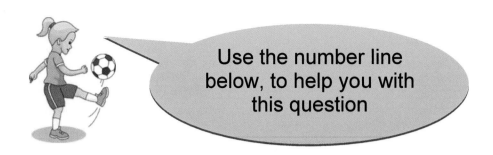

Use the number line below, to help you with this question

If a team wins a league match they get 3 points. If they draw, a match they get 1 point. They get 0 points if they lose. Fill in the number of points under each result. Then add them up.

	Draw	+	Loss		Total
New York	[ ]		[ ]	=	[ ]

	Win	+	Draw		
Los Angeles	[ ]		[ ]	=	[ ]

	Loss	+	Loss		
Seattle	[ ]		[ ]	=	[ ]

Number line

0   1   2   3   4   5   6   7   8   9   10

Enter your score for this page: [ ] — [ ]

If a team wins a league match they get 3 points. If they draw a match, they get 1 point. They get 0 points if they lose. Fill in the number of points under each result. Then add them up.

	Draw	+	Draw	+	Loss		Total
Portland	☐		☐		☐	=	☐

	Win	+	Draw	+	Draw		
Orlando	☐		☐		☐	=	☐

	Draw	+	Win	+	Win		
Dallas	☐		☐		☐	=	☐

Number line

0   1   2   3   4   5   6   7   8   9   10

Enter your score for this page: ☐ — ☐

Patterns. Fill in the next shirt numbers for each team.

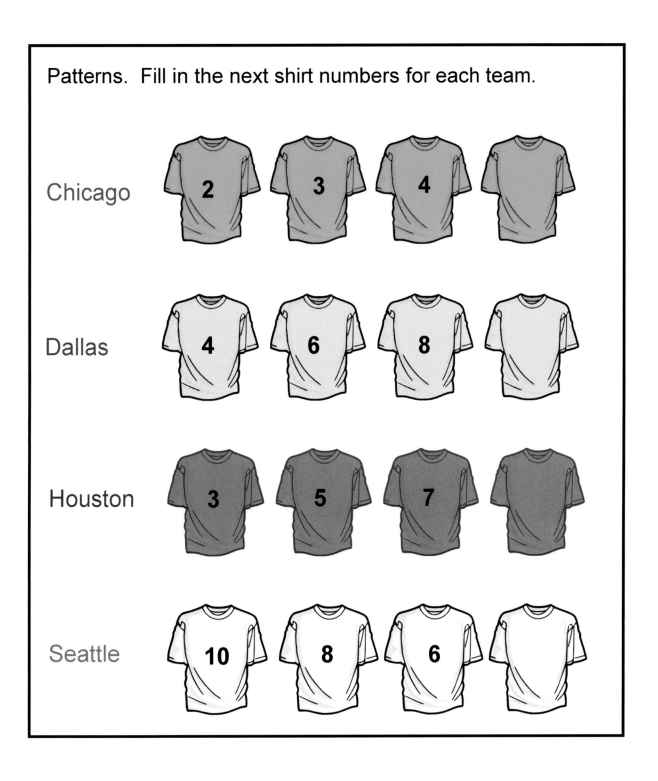

Chicago 2 3 4 ___

Dallas 4 6 8 ___

Houston 3 5 7 ___

Seattle 10 8 6 ___

Enter your score for this page: 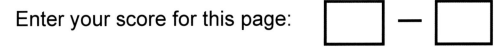 ⬜ — ⬜

13

Draw a line from the word to the correct soccer ball.

Whole	Half	Quarter

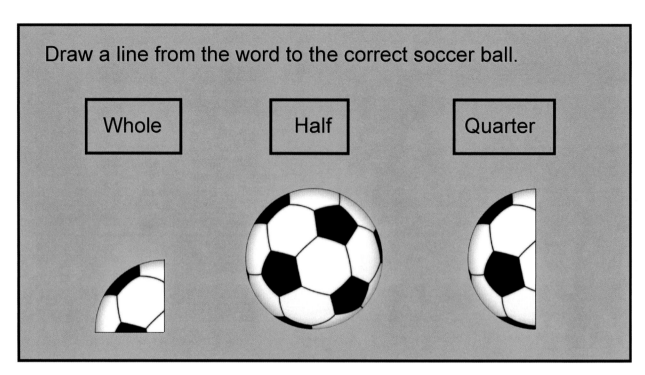

How many soccer balls can you make from the below?

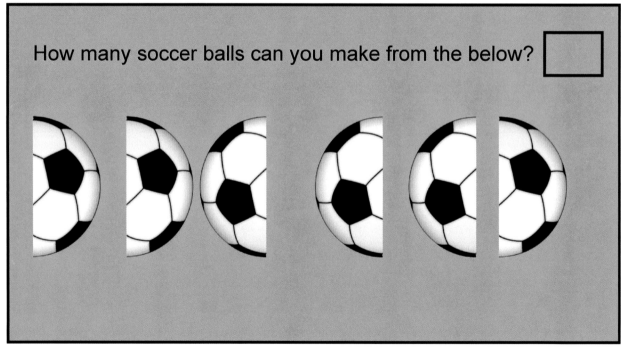

Enter your score for this page:

Write **odd** or **even** in the box next to the shirt number.

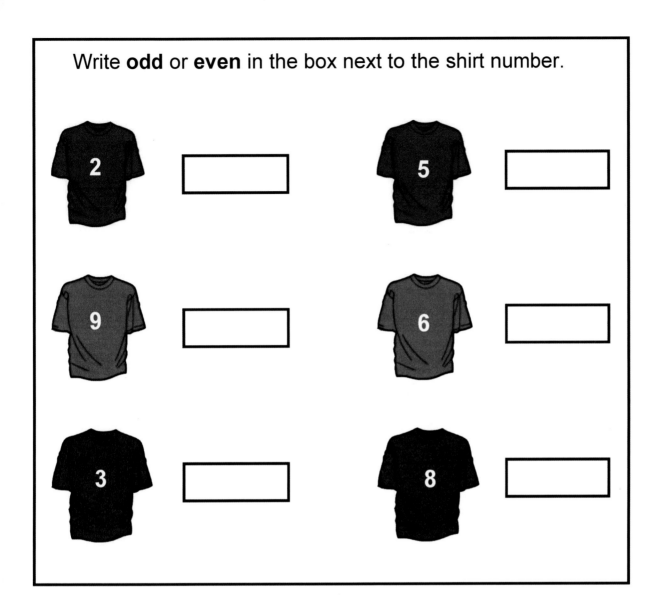

2 ☐

5 ☐

9 ☐

6 ☐

3 ☐

8 ☐

Enter your score for this page: ☐ — ☐

Keep halving the score below

Half of zero is zero

Below are the full-time scores in 4 matches. At half-time the scores were exactly half what the full-time scores were. Fill in the half-time scores below.

Full time   Half - time

0 – 4   ⟹   ☐ – ☐

6 – 0   ⟹   ☐ – ☐

2 – 2   ⟹   ☐ – ☐

4 – 2   ⟹   ☐ – ☐

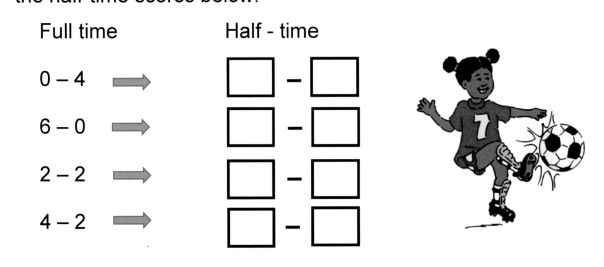

Enter your score for this page: ☐ — ☐

How many teams play in a cup final?

Example: New York v Los Angeles

How many teams play in a semi-final?

Example: New York v Seattle

Los Angeles v Portland

How many teams play in a quarter final?

Example: Dallas v New York

Seattle v Houston

Los Angeles v Orlando

Portland v Chicago

If 2 teams are playing each other in the cup, it's called a 'cup tie'

Enter your score for this page:

If a **cup tie** consists of 2 matches, these are called the 'First Leg' and the 'Second Leg'

Sometimes in a **cup tie**, teams play each other twice, once at home and once away from home. When you add up each team's combined scores this is called the **aggregate score**.

	Home team		Away team
First Leg:	Chicago	4 – 3	New York
Second Leg:	New York	2 – 4	Chicago

How many goals did Chicago score in total? ☐

How many goals did New York score in total? ☐

Complete the blanks below to find out the **aggregate score**:

_____ won by _____ goals to _____

Enter your score for this page: ☐ — ☐

The scores in the other semi-final are below:

	Home team		Away team
First Leg:	Seattle	5 – 3	Orlando
Second Leg:	Orlando	2 – 2	Seattle

Seattle scored a total of ☐ goals

Orlando scored a total of ☐ goals

Complete the blanks below to find out the **aggregate score**:

_____ won by _____ to _____

Enter your score for this page: ☐ — ☐

A soccer team consists of 11 players. As 1 player is always the goalkeeper, this leaves 10 outfield players.

Enter the number of defenders, midfielders and attackers in the boxes.

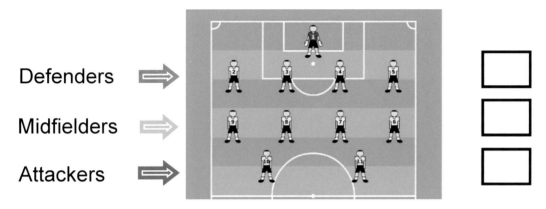

Defenders ⟹ ☐

Midfielders ⟹ ☐

Attackers ⟹ ☐

This is called a 4-4-2 formation.

Fill the boxes for the opposition team.

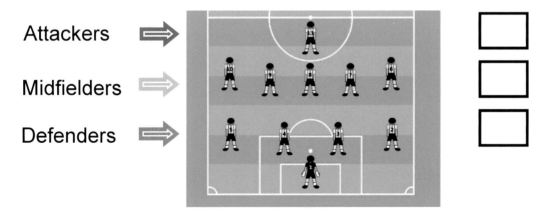

Attackers ⟹ ☐

Midfielders ⟹ ☐

Defenders ⟹ ☐

4 defenders, 5 midfielders, 1 attacker = 4-5-1 formation.

Enter your score for this page: ☐ — ☐

Fill in the number of attackers in the 3 teams below to make sure they all have 10 outfield players.

Defenders		Midfielders		Attackers		Total
4	+	4	+		=	10

Defenders		Midfielders		Attackers		Total
4	+	2	+		=	10

Defenders		Midfielders		Attackers		Total
5	+	3	+		=	10

Number line

0   1   2   3   4   5   6   7   8   9   10

Enter your score for this page: ☐ — ☐

Fill in the number of midfielders in the 3 teams below to make sure they all have 10 players.

Defenders		Midfielders		Attackers		Total
4	+		+	3	=	10

Defenders		Midfielders		Attackers		Total
3	+		+	3	=	10

Defenders		Midfielders		Attackers		Total
4	+		+	2	=	10

Number line

0   1   2   3   4   5   6   7   8   9   10

Enter your score for this page: ☐ — ☐

If a team's last 5 results were Win, Draw, Loss, Win, Draw, then this is written using the initials of the words = WDLWD

Your team's last 10 results were:

LWDLWDLWWW

Enter the number of wins your team got ☐

Enter the number of draws your team got ☐

Enter the number of losses your team got ☐

Now check what the 3 numbers in the boxes add up to.

Number line

0   1   2   3   4   5   6   7   8   9   10

Enter your score for this page: ☐ — ☐

Keep track of the following match score as the goals go in! The first two are completed for you…

	Home		Away
Kick off	0	—	0
The away team quickly score 2 goals	0	—	2
The home team then pull a goal back		—	
The home team get a penalty but miss it!		—	
An away team player scores an **own goal**!		—	

The ref blows the final whistle! Did you get the correct score?

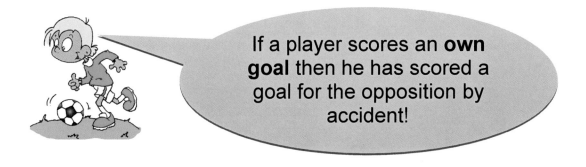

If a player scores an **own goal** then he has scored a goal for the opposition by accident!

How many of the six boxes above did you get right and wrong?

Enter your score for this page: ☐ — ☐

Keep track of the following match score as the goals go in! The first two are completed for you…

	Home		Away
KICK OFF	0	—	0
The home team scores after 10 minutes	1	—	0
The home team then double their lead		—	
The away team's striker scores 2 goals!		—	
HALF-TIME			
An away team player scores an own goal!		—	
Free kick to the home team. He shoots. Goal!!		—	
The home team get a penalty! Goal!!		—	
FULL-TIME			

The referee blows the final whistle. Did you get the correct score?

Enter your score for this page: ☐ — ☐

Columbus decide to buy 2 new players below. How much money have they spent in total?

Player	Cost
Brad Kelly	$1 million
Mick Donovan	$2 million
Total Cost	$

Chicago decide to sell 2 players. How much money do they receive in total?

Player	Amount
Clark Robson	$4 million
Parker Smith	$3 million
Total amount	$

Enter your score for this page: ☐ — ☐

To score a goal you have to find a vertical route to the goal which is made up from **odd** numbers. Can you find the route?

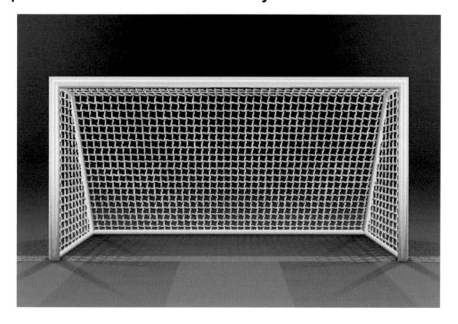

8	4	9	5	2
3	8	9	5	3
2	6	8	3	7
6	5	9	1	9
5	1	4	9	5

Enter 1-0 if you got it right, or 0-1 if you didn't: ☐ — ☐

To score a goal this time you have to find a vertical route to the goal made up from **even** numbers. Can you find the route?

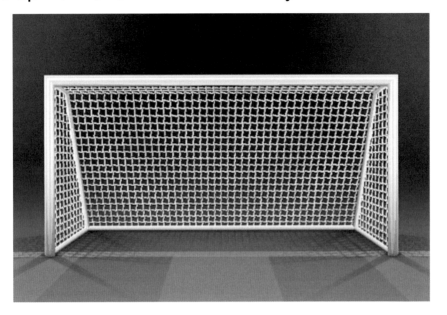

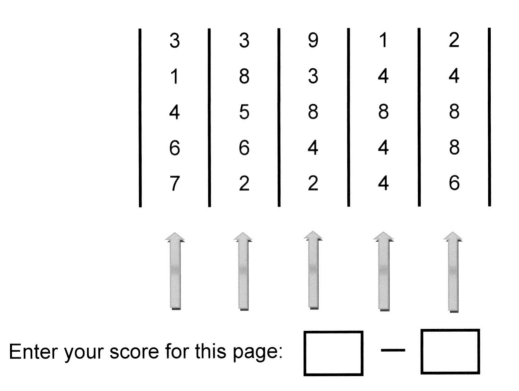

3	3	9	1	2
1	8	3	4	4
4	5	8	8	8
6	6	4	4	8
7	2	2	4	6

Enter your score for this page: ☐ — ☐

The first half of a soccer match lasts 45 minutes. Another way of looking at 45 is in Tens and Units:-

<u>Tens</u>   <u>Units</u>

40 + 5

The second half of a soccer match is also 45 minutes. Again this can be split into Tens and Units:-

<u>Tens</u>   <u>Units</u>

40 + 5

A match consists of the number of minutes in the first half + the number of minutes in the second half. How many is this in total?

Add the Tens for each half: 40 + 40 = ☐

Add the Units for each half: 5 + 5   = ☐

Now add the boxes to find out how long a match lasts ☐

Enter your score for this page: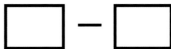

29

In an 11-a-side match, each team has 11 players. How many players are on the pitch in total:-

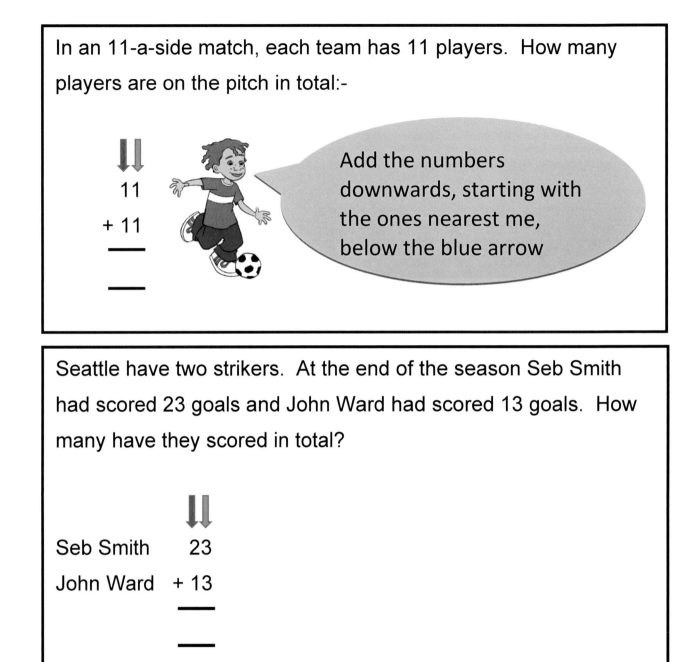

11
+ 11
———

———

Add the numbers downwards, starting with the ones nearest me, below the blue arrow

Seattle have two strikers. At the end of the season Seb Smith had scored 23 goals and John Ward had scored 13 goals. How many have they scored in total?

Seb Smith   23
John Ward   + 13
              ———

              ———

Enter your score for this page: ☐ — ☐

Answers

Page

1 (a) 4, 8, 10   (b) 2, 5, 9, 10

3 (a) 5   (b) 4

4 (a) 8 (b) 14

5 (a) 2, 1, 1 (b) 2, 3, 3

6 Chicago 2 – 3 Seattle

7 (a) New York 3 - 4 Portland   (b) Houston 2 – 3 Dallas

8 (a) Dallas 3 – 1 Portland   (b) Orlando 4 – 2 Seattle

9 (a) 3, 4   (b) 6, 3

10 (a) 4-2, 8-4   (b) 8-0, 0-0, 2-2, 4-4, 2-6

11]   1+0=1,   3+1=4,   0+0=0

12]   1+1+0=2,   3+1+1=5,   1+3+3=7

13] 6, 10, 9, 4

14] (a) Whole = , Half = , Quarter =   (b) ½ + ½ + ½ + ½ +1 = 3

15] 2=Even, 5=Odd, 9=Odd, 6=Even, 3=Odd, 8=Even

16] (a) 2-0, 1-0 (b) 0-2, 3-0, 1-1, 2-1

17] 2, 4, 8

18] 8, 5

19] 7, 5

20] (a) 4, 4, 2 (b) 4,5,1

21] 2, 4, 2

22] 3,4,4

23] 5, 2, 3

24] 1-2, 1-2, 2-2

25] 2-0, 2-2, 3-2, 4-2, 5-2

26] (a) $3 million, (b) $7 million

27] Column 4

28] Column 5

29] 80, 10, 90

30] 22, 36

Books by Adrian Lobley

The Football Maths Book Series

The Football Maths Book

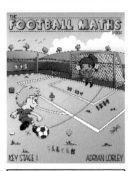

Book 1 in the series
Age 4-7

The Soccer Math Book

US version of The
Football Maths Book
Age 4-7

El libro de matemáticas de fútbol

Spanish version of The
Football Maths Book
Age 4-7

The Football Maths Book
The Re-match!

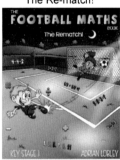

Book 2 in the series
Age 5-8

The Football Maths Book
The Christmas Match

Book 3 in the series
Age 6-8

The Football Maths Book
The Birthday Party

Book 4 in the series
Age 7-8

The 'A Learn to Read Book' Series

A Learn to Read Book:
The Football Match
Age 4-5

A Learn to Read Book:
The Tennis Match
Age 4-5

Made in the
USA
Monee, IL